VAUX LE VICOMTE

Éditions Pro Libris

"Entranced on entrance, the grotto,
The canals, the superb portico
Palatial places that through their beauty birth
A belief it must all be a dream
If Vaux was not of this earth".

Jean de La Fontaine

ÉDITIONS PRO LIBRIS
44 rue Monge
75005 Paris
Tél.: 01 64 99 76 76
Fax: 01 64 99 76 54

Vaux le Vicomte: the north front.

Photographs by Béatrice Lécuyer-Bibal

South front of the Chateau.

Vaux le Vicomte

For over three and a half centuries, the several thousand acres stretching around Vaux le Vicomte have seemed to belong to another time, an unchanging country environment encompassing this masterpiece built in the XVIIth century by three of the greatest French artists of the age, brought together by the taste and discernment of Nicholas Fouquet, the Lord High Treasurer or *"surintendant des Finances"*. The palace and its outbuildings, designed by Louis Le Vau, and its decorations by Charles Le Brun, whose signature suggests that pleasure counted for more than glory, would survive a succession of wars, revolutions and neglect; the gardens were laid out by André Le Nôtre, the first in a series of *"jardins français"* that would be imitated throughout Europe.

This rare survival owes its magic to the effect it has on the sensitivities of each one of us, to the exceptional harmony which sets surfaces against voids, buildings in gardens, and charms the eye and indeed all our senses. But it is also the hard work of four families whose endeavours have allowed us to keep this last great monument to precede the wholesale takeover by official art and that of the court.

And yet its beginnings were dramatic: Nicholas Fouquet would only ever spend a few nights in this palace, symbolising as it did the rise of his career and ambition. The house would never be definitively furnished or finished, but merely filled with furniture and artworks brought in from Paris and Saint Mandé for the occasional family and political festivities. The decorative artisans were still at their work when, on Wednesday August 17th 1661 Fouquet laid on a party of unrivalled magnificence for the King. Yet all unbeknownst to him, Colbert, who harboured a great hatred against for Fouquet, had managed to convince the young Louis XIV - who had just assumed personally the reins of power - to summon Fouquet before a special court, the *"cour d'exception"*; while denying him access to a lawyer and purloining false evidence Colbert requested that Fouquet be condemned to death. With the party over and the guests departed, d'Artagnan had Fouquet arrested at Nantes, on Monday September 5th 1661. The trial would last over three years. But royal plunder would not wait for judgement: all the most precious valuables in Vaux le Vicomte, including some 120 tapestries, hundreds of statues and thousands of orange and box trees, were carted off to the Louvre and to Versailles, both palaces then being enlarged by the young King.

Portrait by Nicholas Fouquet (1615-1680).

At the end of the trial, most of the judges, setting aside the King's orders, delivered the reduced sentence of banishment. The King crushed this ruling and had his former minister thrown into the deepest dungeon in Pignerol: there Fouquet would die after nineteen years in captivity.

Vaux le Vicomte, like Belle-Île, was nevertheless handed back to Madame Fouquet. Her anxiety for her husband, the burden of paying back his debts, together with the huge running costs of the château of Vaux, would have cast down many a soul, but for many years she clung on until finally the death of her eldest son left the family without issue and in 1705 Marie Magdeleine Fouquet resolved to sell the whole, vast, burdensome estate.

The Maréchal de Villars, covered as he then was with glory, bought Vaux le Vicomte without even visiting it. He turned out to be a model landowner who set about restoring the place with a passion: whenever his military campaigns allowed it, he would come here to rest and to amuse himself, surrounded by his friends who appreciated getting away from the strictures of Versailles etiquette and enjoying the gay company of the beautiful Madame de Villars. Invitations to Vaux were much sought after and Voltaire was counted among the regular guests.

The de Villars family only had one son, whose only merit lay in taking on the mantle of his father's glory. Thereby he acquired the reversion of the government of Provence, which he preferred to the Île-de-France and sold Vaux in 1764.

Engraving by Israël Silvestre.

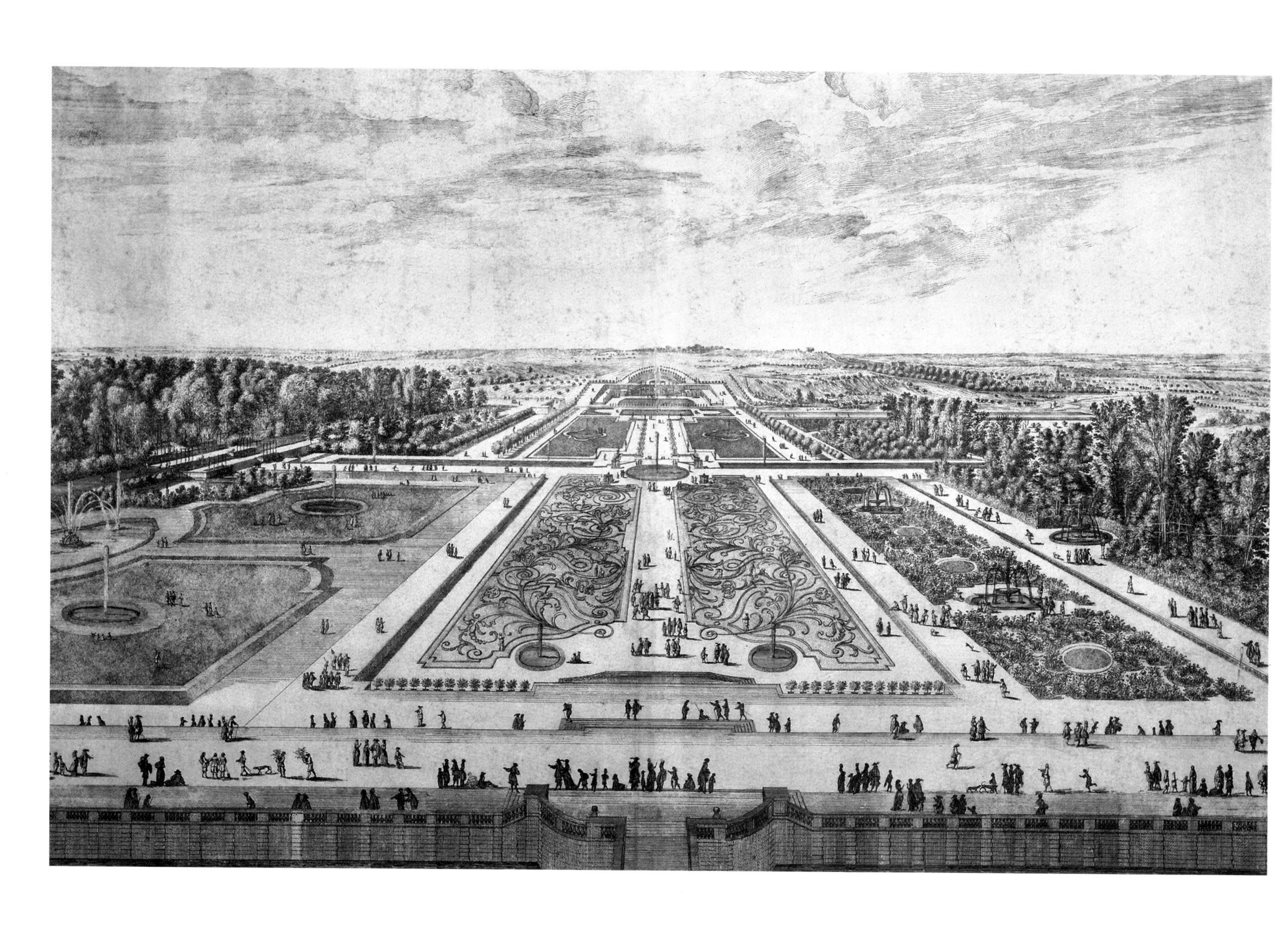

The garden, seen from the chateau, after Israël Silvestre.

The Duke of Praslin, the head of a branch of the Choiseul family, became the new owner. He was Louis XV's Minister for Foreign Affairs, and later became his Navy Minister. Praslin was sober, phlegmatic, reflective and content to introduce a few comforts to the first floor of the chateau. His descendants, who managed the estate with parsimony, yet with generosity to their neighbours, also made their own contribution to the preservation of this archetypal monument during the first years of the revolution. But in 1793, an order was received by the Duchess of Praslin to strip out the chateau to leave it clear for demolition.

With some skill she managed to play for time on the pretext of removing the masterpieces of Le Brun as a gift to the nation, that is to say, the main ceiling canvases and perhaps also certain frescoes were also transposed beforehand. This initiative provoked the zeal of a commission of experts who concluded that the monument should be saved: but they became so wrapped up in their prevarications that their discussions coincided with the end of the revolution and thereby Vaux escaped the revolutionary ideologies of nationalisation or destruction.

There were five successive generations of the Choiseul family, from 1764 to 1875, during which time the monument was neither modified, nor did it receive the necessary attention to its upkeep. In particular the famous formal gardens of Le Nôtre which had been rented out to an estate farmer had disappeared under cultivation and pasture.

In 1847 a family drama put an end to all the hopes of the Choiseul family: the Duke of Praslin murdered his wife Fanny Sebastiani, and then committed suicide. Their eldest son Gaston left Vaux, never to return, and put the estate up for sale by auction in 1875. A rumour went around that Vaux was going to meet the same fate as that of fabulous chateau of Richelieu, and find itself prey to a building materials' merchant who would demolish the buildings and sell it off stone by stone.

It so happened that a youthful and amateur lover of the arts, alerted of the fact by a friend, came upon the abandoned estate prior to the auction. For him it was love at first sight, and on the day of the auction he proved to be the only bidder: it was none other than Alfred Sommier (1835-1908), the grandson of a baker from Villeneuve-sur-Yonne. He set about restoring the buildings, reconstructing the Le Nôtre gardens and refurnishing the château to the highest standards. This titanic undertaking was in great part financed by a personal fortune obtained from his father's sugar refinery, a factory that his father had designed and built with his own hands; Alfred had become the refinery manager at the tender age of eighteen. His son, Edme (1873-1945) continued the work of restoration, but Edme being childless, it was carried on by his nephew, Jean de Vogüé, the eldest son of his sister. With each passing year the work became more difficult, but the mission remained unchanged: to save this masterpiece of the XVIIth century.

This beautiful place opened its gardens to the public in 1947 and the chateau in 1968. Vaux, a listed Historic Building, receives a dwindling number of subsidies and the owner is able to benefit from an income tax regime - controversial in an age of levelling ideology - which allows him to deduct the losses from the use and maintenance of monument in keeping with the degree of accessibility to the public.

And so it is that today those who wish can enjoy Vaux le Vicomte as a major work of period architecture and landscape design, and along a perspective well over a mile long, buildings, embroidered parterres and lawns, reflecting pools and gushing fountains, walks and promenades. But all this also expresses the soul of one of the great patrons of the XVIIth century, Nicholas Fouquet, and those of his friends and protégés, the writers La Fontaine, Corneille, Molière, Pelisson, Scarron, and some of the most eminent artists of the XVIIth century, to whom a young prince, soon to be called the Sun King, would confer the task of building the greatest palace in the world.

Patrice de Vogüé

The chateau, the north-west front, by Israël Silvestre.

The approach road to Vaux le Vicomte: the plane tree drive.

The ironwork gate of the "Cour d'Honneur".

South front of the chateau.

Embroidery in Box hedging: a winter scene under snow.

Bordered lawns, the Triton basin.

Bordered lawns, the Triton basin.

• *The Rape of Europa by Hiolle and Chapu.*

• *Page 19. The chateau south front and outbuildings.*

The bay windows of the Italian salon give onto the garden via a drawbridge.

The south steps leading to the Italian Salon peristyle.

Carved tables above the windows: the squirrel, the symbol of Fouquet and his personal monogram, four interwoven "F" s.

The chateau seen from the Round Basin terrace.

• *Detail of the box hedge "embroidery" (recreated in 1923 by Achille Duchêne).*

• *Page 25. The central perspective over the garden seen from the lantern atop the dome.*

The flowerbeds.

The flowerbeds seen from the dome.

• *A female sphinx peers out of the flowers.*

• *Page 29. A view of various statues that stand near the flowerbeds.*

Cherubs bearing heavily laden baskets; statuary originating from the "château de Maisons".

Cast-iron vases: XVIIth century examples.

• *Cast-iron vases: XVIIth century examples.*

• *Page 34-35. Tigers by Gardet (1863-1939).*

• *Bacchus, XVIIIth century.*

• *Page 36. Lions by Gardet (1863-1939).*

Abundance,
XVIIIth century.

Zephyr and Flora, XVIIIth century.

• *A dolphin in the Couronne ornamental ponds.*

• *Page 41. The Couronne ornamental ponds.*

One of the grotesque masks forming a water spout.

Back-to-back Termes, XVIIth century.

The dry grotto, known today as the Confessional.

XVIIth century statues: autumn, summer.

• *Triton by Peynot (1850-1932).*

• *Page 46. The Reef and the Wave by Loysel (1867-1925).*

Naiad by Peynot (1850-1932).

• *Triton by Peynot (1850-1932).*

• *Page 50-51. Naiad.*

• *A view across the gardens from the Gerbe basin.*

• *Page 52. The Horses of the Sea by Lanson (1851-1898).*

The waterfall basin.

The grotesque masks of the waterfalls.

Promenade along the Poêle canal.

Hercules' drive.

The Poêle canal.

The path skirting round to the east of the Poêle canal.

• *Lion and squirrel by Lespagnandel.*

• *Page 60. The Grottoes designed by Le Nôtre.*

The river god of Ancoeur (by Lespagnandel) and the stepped Grottoes.

The four corners of the world: America by Peynot 1892.

The frog basin.

The "Water-Sheaf".

• *The Farnèse Hercules statue at sunrise.*

• *Page 67. The Farnèse Hercules looks onto the south front of the chateau.*

• *The Farnèse Hercules: the XIXth century realisation of a project by Fouquet.*

• *Page 69. The chateau, as seen in the square reflecting pool.*

The western outbuildings.

The eastern outbuildings.

• *The courtyard serving the stables and the Carriage Museum*

• *Page 73. The quadriga, a roman chariot pulled by four horses.*

Different types of harnessing from the XIXth century.

The sedan chair harnessed by mules.

Wourch in full harness and ready for duty (in trust from the town of Angoulême).

Forge and the old fire pump.

Portals topped by decorative finials.

The moat running in front of the north front of the chateau.

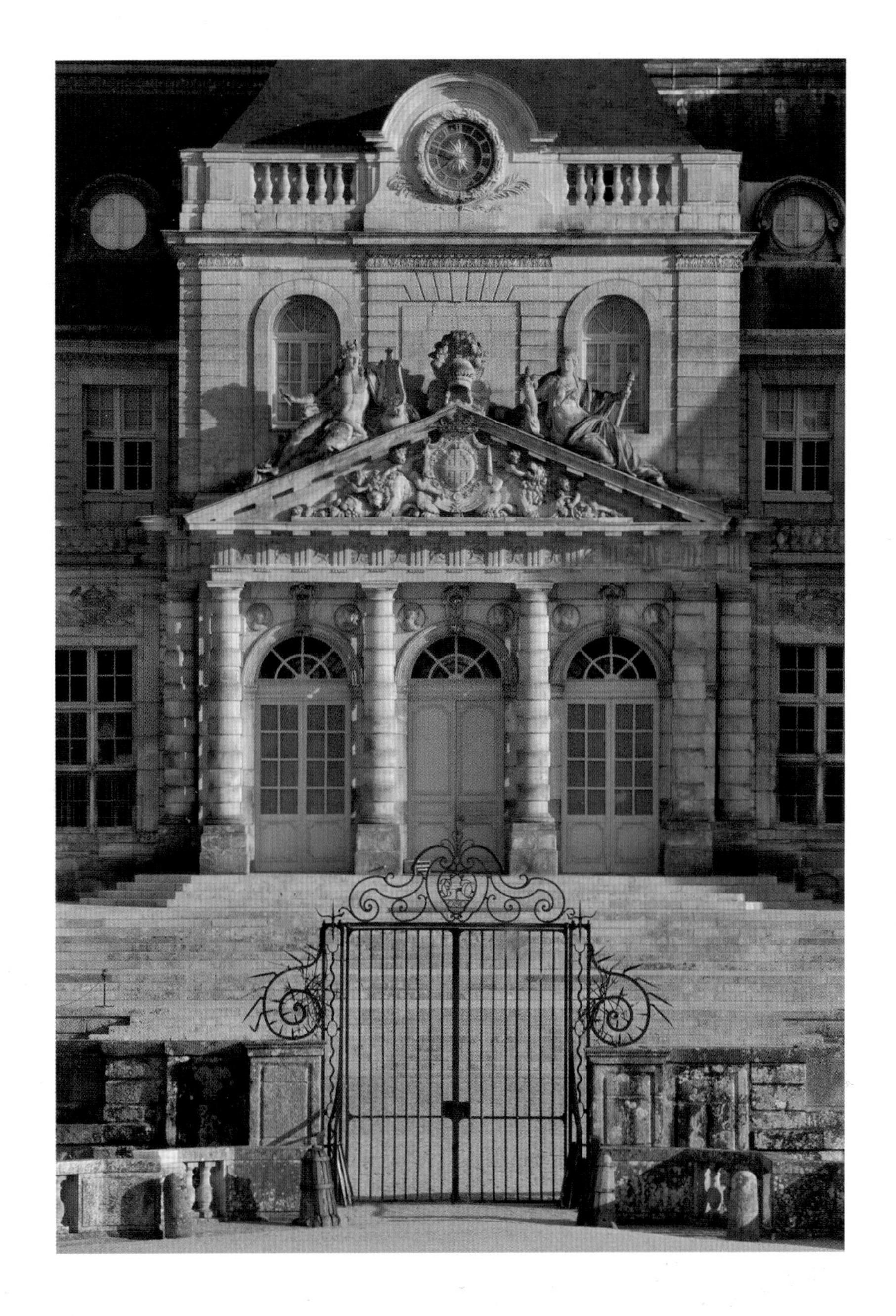

• *Northern peristyle.*

• *Page 80. The chateau and its moat at sunset.*

At Vaux le Vicomte, the formal, ceremonial apartments, the privy apartments, the servants' quarters and the attic floors are all now open to the public.

While the ground floor rooms have never been altered, those on the first floor were modernised by the Praslins' architect Berthier at the end of the XVIIIth century in order to allow for some extra comfort. The considerable collection of furniture which the château enjoys today is the fruit of the Sommier family and their heirs and successors; it reflects the constant and ongoing attempt to place before the visitor the furnishings of the XVIIth century and, preferably, those predating 1661. That was the year that Fouquet was thrown into prison and all his activities as a patron of the arts and as a collector came to an abrupt halt. The recreation of this collection began in 1875, bringing together period furniture, sculpture, paintings and tapestries. The latter were omnipresent when the Lord High Treasurer, Surintendant Fouquet was at the peak of his career, thanks to the personal manufactory that he had set up in Maincy, in the château's parish, where French and Flemish weavers laboured under the orders of Charles Le Brun. After Fouquet's downfall, this industry, along with some Parisian workshops, re-emerged as the Gobelins textile manufactory.

Wooden panel bearing the four interlaced F's pierced by an arrow, Fouquet's personal monogram.

Details of various painted wood panels.

Nicolas Fouquet's bedroom.

Nicolas Fouquet's bedroom: the alcove ceiling.

Madame Fouquet's bath-chamber or cabinet.

• *A window in Madame Fouquet's cabinet.*

• *Portrait painting of Madame Fouquet by the workshop of Charles Le Brun.*

XVIIIth century bath-chamber or "Cabinet de toilette".

A Villars period bed-chamber.

A Praslin bed-chamber.

The eastern landing of the Great Staircase.

The large square bedchamber: Two marble-top tables owned by Nicolas Fouquet.
The Story of Diana: Tapestries after Toussaint Dubreuil.

• *The Lord High Treasurer, Surintendant Fouquet by Charles Le Brun.*

• *A marble of Louis XIV, by a sculptor of the school of Bernini.*

The alcove of the chamber of the Muses, tapestries relating the story of Aminte and Sylvie. A pair of "mazarin" commodes by Boulle. A Savonnerie rug with a black background.

• *Chamber of the Muses: Thalie, the muse of comedy by Charles Le Brun.*

• *Bust of Molière and central ceiling motif.*

The games cabinet and backgammon table.

• *The ceremonial succession of apartments seen from the Hercules antichamber.*

• *Detail of a door panel.*

• *The ceiling of the Hercules antechamber:*
a demi-God before Olympus, by Charles Le Brun.

• *Love and Psyche, decoration in blue monochrome, XVIIth century.*

• *Page 96. The Hercules antechamber.*

The Italian salon at Vaux le Vicomte.

The King's Antechamber: a desk by Boulle and a great Savonnerie carpet with a blue background.

The ceiling of the King's Antechamber: painted around 1835.

The King's Bedchamber.

The ceiling of the King's Antechamber: the god Jupiter, Time carrying up Truth to heaven and the god Mars, paintings by Charles Le Brun and stucco by Legendre.

The King's Cabinet: portrait of the Marshal of Villars by Coypel, and of Louis XV after Van Loo.

The Marshal of Villars's antechamber: his portrait and his archives.

• *The Marshal of Villars's antechamber.*

• *The bathroom ceiling by Visconti (1791-1853).*

• *The Ceiling of the Buffet Room: in the centre, Peace brings abundance; in grey monochrome, the four seasons and in gold and blue, the four elements.*

• *Page 107. General view of the Buffet Room.*

• *The servants' hall.*

• *The wine-cellar.*

• *Reconstruction of the dungeon holding the Man in the Iron Mask.*

The Great Kitchen.

- *A reconstruction of the "fête" held on the August 17th 1661: the musketeers.*
- *Page 111. A reconstruction of the "fête" held on the August 17th 1661.*

Guests in period costume during the "fête du Grand Siècle", the festival celebrating "the Great Century". The south front of the chateau.

A candlelit evening: the gardens before the south front of the chateau.

The south front of the chateau.

The "Festival of Open Air Opera" on the north steps of the chateau.

Christmas nights: the entrance by the "Cour d'Honneur".

• *The Great Railings of the Cours des Bornes, flanked by giant back-to-back "Termes".*

• *Page 118. Fireworks.*

In the same collection

"Chantilly Domaine Princier".

Translation into English by William Jordan.

I would like to thank the Akouna Open Air Opera Association and also to Tristan Duval.

Dépôt légal mars 2009
N° Éditeur: 978-2-908597
ISBN: 978-2-908597-19-6
Imprimeur -Aubin CPI France

www.pro-libris.com
beatrice.bibal1@aliceadsl.fr
prolibris-editeur@wanadoo.fr